Introdu...

Everyone loves teddy bears and cake decorators like me are certainly no exception! Having taught sugarcraft for a number of years, I have found that students really love to make bears for cakes and it is so rewarding to see their enthusiasm and delight as they create their own adorable characters. Making Sugar Teddy Bears is the result of many happy years teaching the art of making sugar teddies. I have aimed to make each step of the process helpful and accessible to everyone, so I hope this book will be a handy guide which can be used again and again. The ten projects cover a range of celebrations including a birthday party, graduation, christening and wedding, so there is plenty to get you started. As you progress through the book, the projects become more advanced and, once you have mastered the basics, you will be able to adapt and create your very own unique teddy bears.

I hope that you will gain as much pleasure from making sugar teddies as I do.

Susan

Susan Griffiths

To my Mother and daughters, Amy and Abbie

Thanks to Beverley, Robert, Jenny and Sarah for all their hard work

First published in March 2003 by b. Dutton Publishing Limited, Alfred House, Hones Business Park, Farnham, Surrey, GU9 8BB.

Copyright: Susan Griffiths 2003

ISBN: 0-9532588-5-8

Publisher: Beverley Dutton

Editor: Jenny Stewart

Designer: Sarah Richardson

Photography: Alister Thorpe

Printed in Spain

Contents

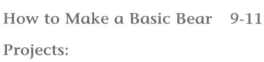

Recipes

All the cakes in this book can be rich fruit cake or a sponge cake such as Madeira. Use the chart opposite as a guide to the quantity of ingredients you will require and cooking times.

Basic Fruit Cake Recipe

Ingredients

450g/1lb mixed fruit

40g/1¹/₂oz glacé cherries, chopped

110g/4oz plain flour

5g/¹/₄ tsp cinnamon

Grated nutmeg

110g/4oz butter

110g/4oz dark brown soft sugar

2 eggs

Grated rind of ¹/₂ orange and ¹/₂ lemon

5ml/1 tsp black treacle

40g/1¹/₂oz chopped almonds

30ml/2tbsp brandy

Preparation

Soak the fruit in the brandy overnight before making the cake.

Method

1. Cream the butter and sugar until light and fluffy. Gradually add the eggs. Fold in the flour and spices. Stir in the fruit, nuts, treacle and citrus fruits. Spoon into prepared tins, spread evenly and depress the centre slightly.

2. Cook in a preheated oven at 140°C/275°F/Gas Mark 1.

3. When cooked, leave in the tin to cool. To store, double wrap in greaseproof paper then in foil.

Basic Madeira Cake Recipe

Ingredients

110g/4oz butter or sunflower margarine

110g/4oz caster sugar

110g/4oz self-raising flour

2 eggs

Method

1. Place all the ingredients into a mixer and beat well. If you require the cake to be firmer than usual, e.g. for a cutting cake, add a little more flour. Place in prepared tin.

2. Cook at 180°C/350°F/Gas Mark 4. For larger cakes, lower the heat and increase cooking time.

3. Upturn the baked cake onto a sugared piece of greaseproof paper and cover with a clean tea towel until cooled.

Ingredient Quantities and Cooking Times

This chart shows all the cake sizes used in the projects in this book, the quantity of ingredients required for each (based on the recipes opposite) and how long the cake should be baked for.

Cake shape	Cake tin size (width x depth)	Multiple of cake recipe	Cooking time: FRUIT	Cooking time: MADEIRA
Round	15 x 5cm/6 x 2$^1/_2$"	1	2$^3/_4$ - 3$^3/_4$ hrs	40 mins
Round	20.5 x 7.5cm/8 x 3"	1$^1/_2$	4 - 4$^1/_2$ hrs	1 hr
Square	15 x 5cm/6 x 2$^1/_2$"	1$^1/_2$	3$^1/_2$ - 4 hrs	50 mins
Oval	20.5 x 16 x 7.5cm/8 x 6$^1/_4$ x 3"	1$^1/_2$	3 - 3$^1/_2$ hrs	1 hr

Cake Covering Quantities

These are the amounts of marzipan and sugarpaste you will need for the sizes of cake in this book.

Cake shape	Cake size	Marzipan/sugarpaste required to cover cake
Round	15cm/6"	455g/1lb
Round	20.5cm/8"	680g/1$^1/_2$lb
Square	15cm/6"	680g/1$^1/_2$lb
Oval	20.5 x 16cm/8 x 6$^1/_4$"	455g/1lb

Materials

Marzipan

Squires Kitchen make a smooth and easy-to-use marzipan, so I find no need to make my own. Whether you choose to buy or make your own marzipan, always ensure it is of high quality, i.e. has a smooth texture and an almond content of at least 23.5%.

Sugarpaste

It is easiest to use a ready-made sugarpaste for cake covering. This is available in a range of colours, but if you wish to colour white sugarpaste, use a cocktail stick to apply paste food colour into a small piece of paste. Knead well, then blend this coloured piece into the remaining sugarpaste. It is always wise to colour more sugarpaste than required as it can be tricky to match the colour again should you need more.

5

SK Mexican Modelling Paste (MMP)

Throughout the book, the side designs and modelled bears have been made using MMP. This is available in a range of colours (below) including Teddy Bear Brown, extremely useful in bear making. Ready-coloured MMP can be mixed together to create numerous colours and strong colours can be toned down by adding white paste. You can also colour MMP with paste colours, as with sugarpaste.

White, Flesh, Teddy Bear Brown, Sunshine, Soft Apricot, Poppy, Rose, Pale Mint, Sky Blue, Wisteria, Slate Grey.

SK Sugar Florist Paste (SFP)

SFP is a stronger paste than MMP which makes it ideal for making sugar flowers and leaves, tiny bows and other delicate items. It can also be used to make moulds for shells, etc.

Royal icing

Squires Kitchen manufacture a high quality royal icing mix which simply requires the addition of water. Make up following the instructions on the packet. However, if you wish to make your own royal icing, the basic recipe is as follows:

1. Pour 75ml/5 tablespoons of water into a clean electric mixing bowl and add 15ml/1 tablespoon dried egg albumen (fortified). Blend until smooth.

2. Weigh out 455g/1lb icing sugar. Set the mixer to a slow speed and gradually mix in approximately half of the icing sugar until the consistency is similar to unwhipped cream.

3. Gradually add the remaining sugar and mix until the icing is smooth and glossy. (You may need slightly more or less icing sugar to achieve the correct consistency.)

Edible food colours

These are available in the following different forms:-

SK Paste Food Colours: use for colouring sugarpaste, MMP, SFP and royal icing. As it is a paste, it does not alter the consistency of the paste/icing as much as liquid colour.

SK Liquid Food Colours: can be used to colour royal icing and are ideal for painting fine details such as eyes and noses.

SK Dust Food Colours: use to highlight cheeks, ears, etc. Can be blended with liquid colours for quicker drying.

SK Metallic Lustre Dust Colours: brush onto cakes to add a sheen. Ideal for bridal outfits and snowy scenes. Can be mixed with a little clear alcohol, confectioners' glaze or cooled, boiled water to create a metallic paint.

SK Edible Glue

A clear glue which is ideal for securing sugar pieces together.

White vegetable fat

Rubbing a little white vegetable fat onto a non-stick board before rolling out modelling paste or flower paste will help to prevent the paste from sticking to the board. It also helps to keep colours vibrant.

Cornflour

Dust onto a non-stick board before rolling out flower paste for frilling and making flowers and leaves. To make a cornflour duster, put some cornflour on a small piece of fine muslin and tie up the corners with an elastic band.

Clear alcohol

A clear spirit, such as gin or vodka, is ideal for diluting dust food colours to make a quick-drying paint.

Equipment

Essential Equipment

Blade and shell tool (PME)

Bone tool (PME)

Cake smoothers

CelSticks: large and small (CC)

Cocktail sticks

Kitchen towel

Paint palette (or saucer)

Paintbrushes: sizes 00 and 2 and small, flat dusting brush

Pastry brush (or similar)

Polythene rolling pins: large and small

Polythene rolling-out board

Round cutters

Scalpel (PME)

Sharp knife

Spaghetti, raw

Sponge

Sugar shaker (for icing sugar)

Teddy head moulds: large, medium and small (SK)

Texturing mats (SK)

Before you start making sugar teddy bears, you will need some basic tools and equipment. The items listed here are needed for most, if not all, the projects in this book, so it is worth investing in these items if you do not already have them. As you work through each project, you will find that there are other items listed at the beginning. These are more specialised items which are only needed for some of the projects. I have given abbreviations of the manufacturers' names beside each item (e.g. SK = Squires Kitchen) and a list of stockists and manufacturers is given on the inside back cover.

Basic Techniques

Covering a Cake Board (Drum)

1. Knead the sugarpaste well and roll out thinly on a non-stick board dusted with icing sugar.

2. Lay the paste over the cake board and roll again. Trim away the excess paste from the board edge using a sharp knife.

3. Using a pastry brush, dampen the top surface of the board around the edge with a little cooled, boiled water, lifting the paste as you do so, to stick the paste to the board.

4. Re-roll the paste and trim the edges again. Cut out the paste from the centre, the same shape as the cake but a little smaller.

Covering a Fruit Cake with Marzipan

1. Brush the edge of the cake top with apricot glaze and position a roll of marzipan around the edge. Flatten with a palette knife.

2. Fill in any holes on the cake surface with small pieces of marzipan.

3. Upturn the cake onto a work board sprinkled with icing sugar. Brush the top and sides of the cake with apricot glaze,

roll out the required amount of marzipan and lay over the cake. Use the palm of your hand to push the marzipan against the cake, then carefully trim to size. Make sure there are no creases along the bottom edge of the cake.

4. Trim away any excess paste at the bottom of the cake.

5. Smooth the marzipan on the top and sides with a pair of cake smoothers.

Covering a Fruit Cake with Sugarpaste

1. Brush a little brandy or clear spirit (e.g. gin or vodka) onto the surface of the marzipanned cake.

2. Take the amount of sugarpaste required and knead well until pliable. Roll out on a non-stick board dusted with icing sugar, ensuring the area of the paste will cover the top and sides of the cake.

3. Lay the paste over the prepared cake. Carefully smooth down the sides using the palm of your hand. Trim and finish with smoothers, in the same way as for the marzipan.

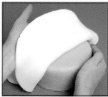

4. Push the cake to the board edge using a smoother onto your hand and place on a covered cake drum.

Covering a Madeira Cake

1. Cut the cake in half horizontally and sandwich with buttercream or a filling of

your choice. Place on a non-stick board and spread a thin, even layer of buttercream over the top and sides of the cake.

2. Cover with sugarpaste using the method opposite and place onto a prepared cake drum.

I always like to trim the board edge with 15mm ribbon in a colour that will complement the cake. Use a non-toxic glue stick to attach the ribbon and make sure the join is at the back.

How to Make a
Basic Bear

Colours

I have used varying tones of Teddy Bear Brown MMP on the bears in this book. These are as follows:

100% Teddy Bear Brown MMP (dark brown, pictured overleaf): birthday bear, ballet bear

50% Teddy Bear Brown MMP + 50% White MMP (mid brown): spring bear, gardening bear, seaside bear, graduation bear, bellboy Bertie

15% Teddy Bear Brown MMP + 85% White MMP (pale brown): christening bears, wedding bears

100% White MMP: Christmas bears

Sizes

There are three sizes of SK Teddy Head moulds available, large, medium and small. The total amount of paste needed for each bear (including body and limbs) is as follows:

Large: 60g/2oz

Medium: 40g/$1^1/_2$oz

Small: 25g/1oz

Use the sizing guides on the inside front cover to proportion the paste, or weigh out the paste as you

go along following the instructions for each bear.

The general principles for making the head, body, arms and legs are the same for all sizes of bear. The instructions for making a large bear head (overleaf) can be adapted for medium and small bears. Remember that you will need to make the head in advance to allow time for the paste to firm before painting.

Large Bear Head

1. Roll 15g of MMP into a ball and then into a cone.

2. Insert the point of the cone into the large teddy head mould. Push the paste well into the mould and round off the back. Texture the back of the head with a texture mat.

If you find that the MMP is sticking to the mould, rub a little white vegetable fat in the palm of your hand when making the cone for the head. This will make the surface of the paste less sticky and easier to remove from the mould.

3. Ease the head out of the mould by gently pulling the paste out from the neck end. Try not to bend the mould as it will change the shape of the head. Re-shape the ears by pushing a bone tool into each one, then push a short piece of raw spaghetti (approximately 5cm/2") halfway into the head. Place in a polystyrene block to firm.

4. Repeat this method until you have enough heads to complete the project. It is always a good idea to make spares as well!

5. Allow to dry. Leaving the paste in a warm place such as an airing cupboard will speed up the drying process.

Painting a Bear Head

1. Mix a small amount of SK Snowflake and Nasturtium dusts together on a piece of kitchen towel. Dust the cheeks and ears.

2. Mix some SK Edelweiss dust and alcohol in a paint palette to make a thick white paint. Paint on the whites of the eyes and a tip on the nose with a no. 2 brush.

3. Mix some SK Bulrush Liquid Colour with Edelweiss dust. Paint the nose and mouth with a no. 00 brush. Leave the white tip on the nose showing.

4. Paint on the eyes with SK Blackberry Liquid Food Colour, leaving the whites of the eyes showing.

Liquid and dust food colours will dry out completely, so are ideal for this purpose. Paste colours do not usually dry out completely so are best avoided. To prevent excess paint running down the face, blot the excess liquid from the paintbrush onto kitchen towel.

Basic Large Bear Body

The principles for making the body and limbs are also the same for any bear. However, when you are dressing the bears, you will notice that the methods vary and you may not need to make the entire basic bear first. (For example, the birthday bear does not require a basic body and legs as the clown suit is made in one piece.)

1. Roll 25g of MMP into a ball. Place between the texture mats and roll into a cone. Flatten the top and push your fingers into the sides where the legs will fit.

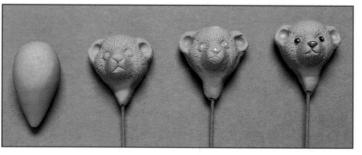

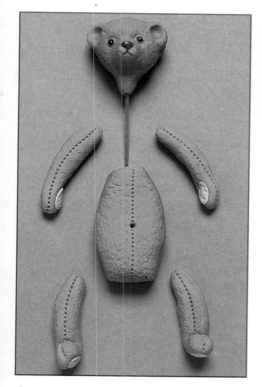

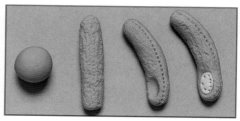

stitching down the centre of each leg.

2. Using your little finger, turn up the bottom third of each leg to form a foot. Hollow out the sole of the foot slightly using a bone tool, then glue a tiny pad of paste into the hollow. Mark stitching on the feet using a small CelStick.

3. Glue the legs into position.

4. To make the arms, roll 8g of MMP into a ball and cut in half. Roll each half between the texture mats into a cylinder.

5. To create paws, roll the end of the paste between your thumb and index finger. Indent with a bone tool, glue in tiny pads and mark stitching. Place each arm on its side and mark stitching.

6. Glue the arms in place at the shoulders.

When making figures, it is easier to work on a small cake board or cake card as this can be moved around easily and can be put to one side for drying. Once firm, the figure can be placed on the cake.

2. Mark stitching down the front and back using a stitching wheel. Make a navel using a large CelStick.

3. Twist the large CelStick into the top of the body.

Arms and Legs

1. To make the legs, roll 10g of MMP into a ball and cut in half. Roll each half between the texture mats, first into a ball and then into a cylinder shape. Mark

Dressing Bears

The great thing about a sugar bear is that it can be dressed for any occasion. In each of the projects which follow, I have listed all the specialist materials and equipment required and how to decorate each cake. This is followed by full instructions on how to dress the bear or bears for each special occasion.

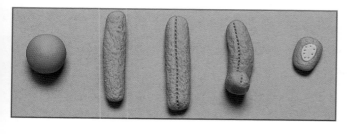

Clowning Around

Materials

15cm/6" square cake

800g/1³/₄lb white sugarpaste

SK Mexican Modelling Paste
(MMP):

75g/2¹/₂oz Poppy

100g/3¹/₂oz Sunshine

25g/1oz Teddy Bear Brown

SK Paste Food Colour: Blackberry

Equipment

23cm/9" square cake drum

Alphabet cutter set: small

Strip cutter: 7mm
(JC)

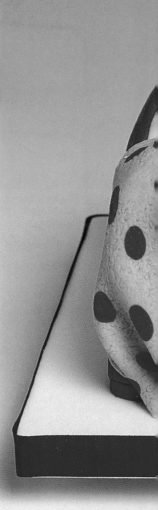

Method

1. Cover the board and cake with white sugarpaste. Position the cake centrally on the board.

2. Cut 7mm wide strips of Poppy MMP using a ribbon cutter and attach to the four sides and top edge of the cake with edible glue.

3. Cut out the letters required from Poppy and Sunshine MMP and attach to the four sides at an angle.

4. Make the birthday bear (see page 14). Place on the cake.

5. To make the blanket, roll out some Sunshine MMP on a non-stick board greased with white fat. Place balls of Poppy MMP onto the paste and roll again. Press between two texture mats. Drape over one corner of the cake.

6. Model the duck from Sunshine MMP. For the eyes, dip a cocktail stick into Blackberry Paste Food Colour and mark dots on the paste. Secure in place.

7. Roll two coloured balls, cut both into quarters, then glue back together using alternate colours. Secure on the cake.

Birthday Bear

1. Model the head from 15g of Teddy Bear Brown MMP and paint on the features.

2. For the body and legs, mould 25g of Poppy MMP into an elongated cone then do the same with 25g of Sunshine MMP. Roll the top ends together and hollow out the wide ends using a bone tool. Bend into a sitting position and mark creases with a blade tool.

3. For the arms use 15g each of Poppy and Sunshine MMP. Model smaller cones, hollow out the ends as before, then bend to shape and mark creases.

4. Thinly roll out some Poppy MMP and cut out two 2.5cm circles. Frill round the edge with a cocktail stick, dusting the board and paste with a little cornflour to prevent the paste sticking. Repeat with Sunshine MMP. Attach to the arms and legs, alternating the colours.

5. For the paws, take two pea-sized pieces of Teddy Bear Brown MMP and roll into cones between two texture mats. Indent with a bone tool and attach pads of Sunshine MMP. Mark stitches using a small CelStick. Glue into the arms and

attach the arms to the body with edible glue.

6. Cut out three 3cm MMP circles for the collar, one Poppy and two Sunshine. Frill and attach.

7. Twist a large CelStick into the top of the body. Brush a little edible glue into the hole and insert the head with a gentle twisting movement.

8. Cut and frill two 2.5cm circles for the hat. Mould a pea-sized amount into a cone for the top of the hat, glue the pieces onto the head and attach pom-poms.

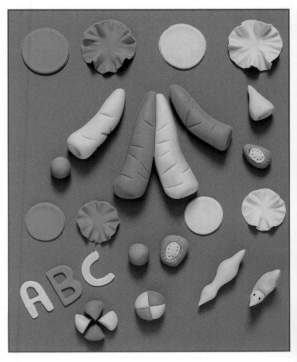

14

Ballet Dreams

Materials

15cm/6" round cake

680g/1¹/₂oz white sugarpaste

SK Mexican Modelling Paste
(MMP):

30g/1oz Rose

60g/2oz Teddy Bear Brown

30g/1oz White

SK Metallic Lustre Dust Colour:

Snowflake

Royal icing

Equipment

23cm/9" round cake drum

Greaseproof paper

Piping bag

Piping nozzle:

no. 43

Scriber

Method

1. Add a small amount of Rose MMP to the white sugarpaste to make a pale pink colour. Cover the board and cake.

2. Make a template for the scallops from greaseproof paper (see Babe in Arms page 36). Use a scriber to mark out the six scallops on the side of the cake.

3. Pipe a shell around the bottom edge of the cake with firm royal icing.

4. Pipe a herringbone effect along the scallop.

Mini Roses

1. Mix together 20g each of White and Rose MMP. This will give you enough paste for the roses and for dressing the bear.

2. Roll a tiny sausage of the pink MMP and flatten along the top edge. Roll up to form the bud, then turn back the very edge of the paste. Make six of these and attach to the top of the scallops with royal icing.

3. Pipe a tiny leaf either side by cutting a small hole in the tip of the piping bag.

To Finish

Make the ballet bear (see page 16) and position on the cake. Dust the dress, shoes and roses with Snowflake Metallic Lustre Dust.

15

Ballet Bear

1. Prepare the head from 15g of Teddy Bear Brown MMP.

2. Model the body from 25g of Teddy Bear Brown MMP and place on a cake card to dress.

3. Make the legs, then attach pads to the feet made from the pink MMP.

4. Roll out a strip of pink paste for the leg warmers, texture between two mats and cut to size for the two legs. Turn down the top edge and mark along the bottom edge with a blade tool. Glue to the legs with the join at the back and position against the body.

5. Cut two pink strips for the bodice straps and glue in place.

6. Cut a rectangle measuring 7 x 2cm for the bodice. Position with the join at the back and mark stitching with a small CelStick.

7. To make the skirt, cut out three 5.5cm circles, two white and one pink. Work on one at a time, starting with white, then pink, then white, and cover the others with cling film to stop the paste drying out. Cut a 2.5cm circle from the centre, frill with a cocktail stick and cut to form a strip.

Make three pleats along the top edge and glue to the body with the join at the back. Once you have secured all three layers, make stitch marks on the bear with a small CelStick.

8. Model the arms, add pink pads and glue in place.

9. Attach the head. For the headband, position a tiny strip of White MMP under the ears and over the head with the join at the back.

10. Roll three very tiny rose buds (see page 15) and attach with edible glue.

11. Make the ballet shoes from cones of paste indented with a bone tool. Cut strips for the ribbon ties and secure in place.

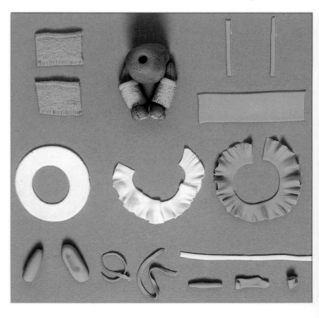

Spring Time

Materials

20cm/8" round cake

910g/2lb white sugarpaste

SK Mexican Modelling Paste (MMP):

35g/1$\frac{1}{4}$oz Teddy Bear Brown

130g/4 $\frac{1}{2}$oz White

SK Sugar Florist Paste (SFP):

20g/$\frac{3}{4}$oz White

SK Paste Food Colours: Daffodil, Leaf Green and Lilac

SK Dust Food Colours: Edelweiss and Rose

Royal icing

Equipment

28cm/11" round cake drum

Blossom plunger cutter set (FMM)

Dresden tool (PME)

Firm sponge

Garrett frill cutter (OP)

Piping bags

Stitching wheel (PME)

Method

1. Colour the white sugarpaste with SK Lilac Paste Food Colour. Roll out and cover the board and cake. Place the cake centrally on the board.

2. Colour some royal icing SK Leaf Green, place in a piping bag and cut a small hole in the end. Pipe around the base of the cake, then brush the icing up the sides using a dry brush to achieve a grass effect.

3. Make the spring bear (see page 20) and place on the cake.

Blossoms

1. Rub a little white fat onto a non-stick board. Knead a little White SFP and roll out thinly.

2. Dust some cornflour onto the surface of the board below the paste.

18

3. Push the plunger blossom into the paste and twist slightly to cut out the blossom shape. Lift the cutter, ensuring the blossom is inside, then rub your finger over the cutter to smooth the edges of the paste.

4. Plunge the blossom onto a firm piece of sponge and leave to dry.

5. Continue making blossoms using three cutters to create different sizes.

Rabbit

1. Roll a large pea-sized piece of White MMP between two texture mats into a cone. Flatten the top slightly and push in a piece of spaghetti. Place in an upright position.

2. Colour a tiny piece of paste Lilac. Roll out and cut out a 3.5cm circle. Frill, then cut a cross in the centre and glue to the body.

3. Texture tiny cylinders of paste for the legs, bend the feet up and mark three indentations. Glue to the body.

4. Texture the arms and attach to the body.

5. Model the head into an oval between texture mats and indent the eyes with a small CelStick. Roll two small cones for the ears, texture and indent with a Dresden tool. Paint the eyes, mouth and nose. Dust the cheeks, feet, paws and ears with a mixture of Rose and Edelweiss Dust Food Colours.

To Finish

1. Using a sponge, stipple some Leaf Green royal icing onto the top edge of the cake and board edge.

2. Position the blossoms and pipe Daffodil coloured royal icing in the centres.

3. Pipe dots of white royal icing onto the bear's dress and hat frill.

4. Pipe frilled sleeves on the rabbit and dress trim. Attach three tiny blossoms to the rabbit head and pipe leaves around them.

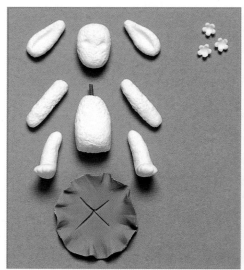

Spring Bear

1. Blend 30g of White MMP with 30g of Teddy Bear Brown MMP to create a mid brown colour. Prepare the head from 15g of the paste.

2. Model the body from 25g of the mid brown paste and place on a cake card to dress.

3. Make the legs then add pads of Teddy Bear Brown MMP.

4. Roll out some White MMP. Cut two strips 8 x 1cm, frill, pleat and attach to the legs with the join at the back. Glue the legs in place.

5. Using a Garrett frill cutter with the medium centre in place, cut out the petticoat. Frill and cut to form a strip. Make three pleats along the top edge. Attach to the lower part of the body with the join at the back.

6. Colour 50g of White MMP with Daffodil Paste Food Colour. Cut a strip 10 x 2.5cm for the bodice, make three pleats along the top edge and glue to the top of the body.

7. For the overskirt, frill and cut a Daffodil yellow Garrett frill. Roll a stitching wheel along the top edge. Attach to the body at waist height.

8. Take two pea-sized pieces of Daffodil paste for the puff sleeves, roll into cones and hollow out the wide end of each with a bone tool. Mark from the inside out with a blade tool.

9. Cut tiny strips of White MMP, frill and pleat. Glue to the inside of the puff sleeves.

10. Make arms from the mid brown paste then add Teddy Bear Brown

MMP for the pads. Glue the sleeves to the arms and attach to the dress.

11. For the collars, roll out some White MMP, cut out two 3.5cm circles and frill. Place in position and re-open the neck with a large CelStick.

12. To make the bonnet, roll a ball of Daffodil paste and flatten the underneath, keeping the top rounded. Mark the edge with a blade tool. Cut a strip 13 x 1.5cm, frill one edge using a cocktail stick and pleat. Attach to the bonnet, leaving a small gap at one end. Glue to the head with the gap at the bottom. Push the head into position and secure with edible glue.

13. Attach two strips of White MMP for the bonnet ties.

Green Fingers

Materials

20 x 15cm/8 x 6" oval cake

910g/2lb white sugarpaste

SK Mexican Modelling Paste (MMP):

50g/1³/₄oz Pale Mint

60g/2oz Teddy Bear Brown

25g/1oz White

25g/1oz Wisteria

Squires Kitchen Sugar Florist
Paste (SFP):

15g/¹/₂oz White

SK Paste Food Colour: Bulrush

SK Pollen-Style Dust Food Colour:
Russet

Royal icing

Equipment

23 x 28cm/9 x 11" oval cake
drum

Blossom plunger cutter set
(FMM)

Cutting wheel
(PME)

Dresden tool
(PME)

Method

1. Colour the white sugarpaste with Leaf Green Paste Food
   Colour. Cover the board and cake. Texture all over the
   surface with a texture mat to create a grass effect.

2. Roll a number of sausages from Pale Mint MMP, varying
   the widths. Glue to the bottom edge of the cake and
   mark with a Dresden tool. Make stalks for the front of the
   cake.

3. Colour a little White SFP with Daffodil Paste Food Colour
   and make a number of blossoms. Glue to the cake.

4. Make the gardening bear (see page 24) and secure in
   place on the cake.

22

Flowerpots, Trug and Garden Accessories

1. For the flowerpots and trug, blend equal quantities of Poppy and Teddy Bear Brown MMP together. You will need approximately 30g of paste.

2. Roll cones of paste for the flowerpots. Roll the wide ends along the edge of a board to create a ridge. Hollow out the centres using a bone tool. Make pots in varying sizes and place around the cake.

3. Make the trug and fill with vegetables.

4. Make the other accessories (gardening gloves, trowel, etc.) as shown and secure in place.

To Finish

1. Sprinkle some Russet Pollen Dust in the flowerpots and over the potatoes.

2. Dust the bear's hat, trousers and boots with Bulrush Dust Food Colour.

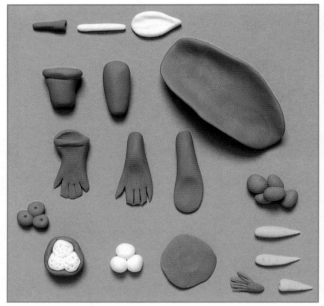

Gardening Bear

1. Blend 15g of White MMP with 15g of Teddy Bear Brown MMP to make a mid brown colour. Prepare the head using 15g of the paste.

2. To make the trousers, roll a tapered sausage from 25g of Teddy Bear Brown MMP and cut lengthways down the middle to separate the legs. Mark creases and bend into a sitting position. Place on a cake card to dress.

3. To make the wellington boots, divide 10g of Pale Mint MMP in half. Roll each piece into a sausage, indent one end

with a bone tool, then bend up the foot at the other end. Insert into the trouser leg and secure with edible glue. Mark the heel with a blade tool.

4. To make the jumper, mould a cone from 20g of Wisteria MMP. Flatten the top and hollow out the wide end with a bone tool. Mark creases and glue to the trousers. Open up the top using a large CelStick.

5. For the sleeves, roll two pea-sized pieces of Wisteria MMP into cones. Indent the wide ends and glue to the jumper.

6. Make arms from mid brown MMP and add Teddy Bear Brown pads.

7. Cut out a 3.5cm circle from Wisteria MMP for the collar. Cut a 'V' from the front and secure in place. Open up the top with a CelStick and position the head.

8. To make the hat, blend together some White and Teddy Bear Brown MMP and add a little Sunflower Paste Food Colour to make a straw colour. (You will need approximately 10g of paste.) Roll into a ball, flatten the edges and indent the underside. Texture

with a mat and roll a cutting wheel over the surface. Glue to the head, bending the hat down at the front.

9. Cut out a pocket for the trousers and patches for the sleeve and hat. Secure in place with edible glue.

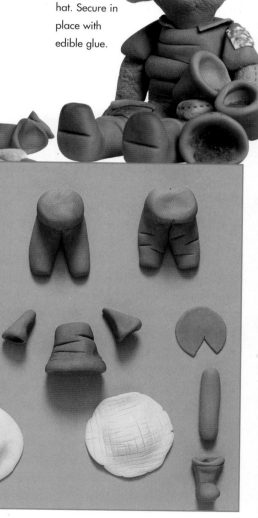

At the Seaside

Materials

20cm/8" round cake

910g/2lb white sugarpaste

SK Mexican Modelling Paste (MMP):

20g/3/4oz Pale Mint

40g/1½oz Poppy

40g/1½oz Teddy Bear Brown

120g/4oz White

50g/1¾oz Wisteria

Squires Kitchen Sugar Florist Paste (SFP)

60g/2oz White

SK Paste Food Colours: Blackberry,

Desert Storm and Sunflower

SK Pollen-Style Dust Food Colour: Pale Golden

Royal icing

Equipment

28cm/11" round cake drum

Shells

Method

1. Colour the white sugarpaste Sunflower yellow. Cover the board and emboss with a texture mat.

2. Cover the cake and position towards the back of the covered board. Texture in the same way.

3. Make the bears (see page 28). Position on top of the cake.

4. Colour some royal icing with Sunflower Paste Food Colour. Dab with a brush around the board, the lower edge of the cake and the top of the cake. Whilst the icing is wet, sprinkle with Pale Golden Pollen Dust.

Shells

1. Make moulds from real shells using White SFP. Clean and dry the shells thoroughly. Mould a small ball of paste, dust with cornflour and push onto the shell. Remove immediately

and leave to dry on a piece of sponge.

2. To make the sugar shells, roll some White MMP into a tiny ball, push into the mould, remove and leave to dry.

3. Dust the MMP shells with a little Desert Storm Dust Food Colour. You will need to make around ten altogether.

Buckets, Towels, Duck and Balls

1. Colour a small amount of White MMP with Sunflower Paste Food Colour. Model buckets in Poppy MMP and Sunflower MMP. Fill the top with royal icing and sprinkle with Pale Golden Pollen Dust.

2. Mix 20g of Pale Mint MMP with 20g of White MMP. Roll out the paste, cut to size for the towels and texture with a mat. Make another one in the same way from Poppy MMP.

3. Make two balls from Wisteria MMP and Poppy MMP.

4. Model the duck. Dip a cocktail stick into Blackberry Paste Food Colour and mark on the eyes.

To Finish

Arrange all the pieces around the bears and board. Once you are happy with the arrangement, glue in place.

Seaside Bears

Blend 30g of White MMP with 30g of Teddy Bear Brown MMP. Using the sizing guides (inside front cover), make a large head for the boy and a medium head for the girl. Paint as desired.

Boy

1. Roll a tapered sausage from 25g of Wisteria MMP for the trousers. Cut length-ways down the middle to separate the legs then bend them up and position the cut edges at the back. Mark creases and hollow out the ends of the legs using a bone tool. Place on a cake card to dress.

2. To make the top, mould a cone from 15g of White MMP. Flatten the top and hollow out the wide end with a bone tool. Mark creases then glue to the top of the trousers. Open up the top with a large CelStick.

3. Roll cylinders of paste for the long sleeves, hollow out the ends and mark creases and cuffs.

4. Model the paws and add Teddy Bear Brown pads. Glue the paws to the arms and secure to the body.

5. Model the legs and attach to the body.

6. Cut out a white collar using the template (see page 48). Attach in place.

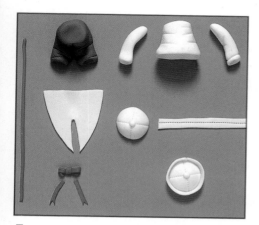

7. For the hat, flatten a pea-sized ball of paste into a circle approximately 3cm in diameter. Hollow out the underside with a bone tool. Mark stitching and glue a tiny ball of paste to the centre. Cut out a strip for the rim measuring approximately 9 x 1cm. Mark stitching through the centre. Glue to the hat with the join at the back.

8. Cut out a thin strip of Poppy MMP for the trim on the collar and make a tiny bow.

9. Finish off the boy bear by adding a tiny white arm patch.

Girl

1. Model a medium-sized body from the mid brown MMP.

2. Mould cones of Wisteria MMP for the pantaloons. Hollow out the wide end and mark a frill effect with a blade tool. Glue to the body.

3. Model the legs and attach to the pantaloons.

4. For the skirt, roll out some Wisteria MMP and cut out a 5cm circle. Cut a 2cm circle from the centre. Make four pleats in the centre, ease over the body and glue into position.

5. Cut a 3 x 4cm rectangle from Wisteria MMP for the top. Place over the body, leaving space to insert the arms.

6. Make the trim for the dress and sleeves from White MMP and glue in place.

7. Make the arms from the mid brown MMP and attach in place.

8. For the hat, roll a tiny pea-sized ball of paste and hollow out the underside. Cut out a 4cm circle and frill the edge. Glue to the ball of paste and mark creases from the edge to the centre.

9. Cut off the ears from the medium head and glue the hat in place. Secure the head on the body.

10. Make a little bow for the front from two cones of paste with a strip across the centre. Mark creases and glue to the hat.

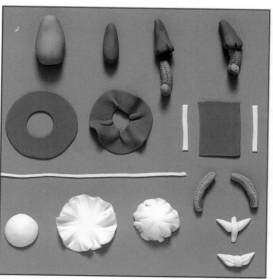

Graduation Party

Materials

15cm/6" square cake

910g/2lb white sugarpaste

SK MMP:

35g/1¹/₄oz Teddy Bear Brown

55g/2oz White

10g/¹/₄oz Wisteria

SK Sugar Florist Paste (SFP):

50g/1³/₄oz Black

SK Liquid Food Colours:
Holly/Ivy and Poinsettia

SK Dust Food Colour: Desert Storm

SK Food Colour Pen:
Blackberry

Royal icing

Equipment

23cm/9" square cake drum

Alphabet cutter set: small

Bow cutter:
small (JC)

Ruler

Method

1. Cover the board with white sugarpaste and leave to firm.

2. For the large books add an extra piece of sugarpaste to one side of the cake. The paste should be the same width and height of the cake and measure approximately 2cm deep.

3. Cover the whole cake with white sugarpaste. Before the paste dries, mark the two books using a ruler and blade tool.

4. Dilute Holly/Ivy and Poinsettia Liquid Food Colours in a little clear alcohol and paint the books using a large brush.

5. Dust the book pages with Desert Storm Dust Food Colour.

6. Roll out some Wisteria MMP and cut out 'Well Done' using the alphabet cutters. Glue the letters to the book.

7. Make the graduation bear (see page 32).

Mortar Boards, Books and Scroll

1. To make the mortar boards, roll out some Black SFP. Cut three 2.5cm squares and leave to firm on a piece of sponge. Roll three pea-sized balls of paste for the hat bases. Hollow out with a bone tool and attach to the squares with a little royal icing. Make tassles from Wisteria MMP and glue in place. Position one of the mortar boards on the bear's head.

2. For the scroll, roll up an oblong of White MMP. Attach a blue strip and position in the bear's arms.

3. To make the small books, roll a sausage of White MMP and pinch out the edges. Mark the pages and centre fold with a blade tool. Dust with Desert Storm and use a Blackberry Food Pen for the lettering.

To Finish

Position the bear on the cake and arrange the books around him. Attach the mortar boards and more books on the edges of the cake board.

Graduation Bear

1. Blend 30g of White MMP with 30g of Teddy Bear Brown MMP. Prepare the head.

2. Make the body, legs and arms using the large size guides. Texture between two texture mats and secure the pieces together. Place the bear on a cake card to dress.

3. Roll out some Wisteria MMP thinly and cut a tiny strip for the tie.

4. Cut out a bow tie using the small bow cutter. Turn the centre piece of the bow over and glue the ends into the middle. Place the top piece of the bow across the centre and glue at the back. (The tail ends of the bow will not be needed.)

5. Wrap the strip around the bear's neck, attaching at the front. Glue the bow tie in place.

6. Knead some Black SFP well before rolling out. Cut out the cloak using the template (page 48). Fold under the lower edge and sides and pleat along the top edge. Wrap the cloak around the bear, draping it over his arms.

7. Add a mortar board, scroll and books, as described above.

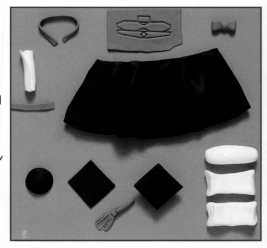

32

Bellboy Bertie

Materials

15cm/6" round cake

680g/1lb 8oz white sugarpaste

SK Mexican Modelling Paste (MMP):

30g/1oz Poppy

30g/1oz Slate Grey

110g/4oz Teddy Bear Brown

50g/1³/₄oz White

40g/1¹/₂oz Wisteria

SK Sugar Florist Paste (SFP):

25g/1oz Black

SK Paste Food Colours: Bulrush and Daffodil

SK Dust Food Colours: Bulrush and Edelweiss

Equipment

23cm/9" round cake drum

Bubble wrap (cleaned)

Button tools (HP)

Method

1. Colour the sugarpaste brown with Bulrush Paste Food Colour.

2. Cover the cake board and emboss the surface with clean, popped bubble wrap. This will give a cobblestone effect.

3. Cover the cake and place towards the back of the board. Emboss the top and sides with the bubble wrap.

4. Dust in places with Bulrush Dust Food Colour.

5. Make the two bellboy bears (see page 34).

Tiny Golly, Suitcases and Hat Boxes

1. Using minute pieces of paste, follow the stage work to make the golly.

2. Make three suitcases from 55g from Teddy Bear Brown MMP weighing 25g, 20g and 10g. Mark the joins with a blade tool, then attach tiny hinges and handles.

3. Using 40g of Wisteria MMP, model one large and one small hat box. Mark out the lid and side design with a blade tool. Attach a red handle to each one.

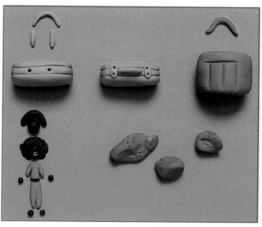

To Finish

1. Place the bears in position on the cake. Lay the golly in the arms of the medium bear. Place two suitcases and a small hat box around them.

2. Make pebbles from Slate Grey MMP and lay them around the board. Place the suitcase and large hat box near the front of the cake on the board.

3. Mix together some Edelweiss Dust Food Colour, Daffodil Paste Food Colour and clear alcohol in a paint palette. Use a fine brush to paint Bertie's coat trimmings, the spots on golly and the hat boxes.

Bellboy Bears

Blend 50g of White and 50g of Teddy Bear Brown MMP. Prepare large and medium heads using the sizing guides (see inside front cover).

Bertie

1. Model a large body and place on a cake card to dress.

2. Cut out a 6cm circle of Black SFP. Wrap around the lower part of body and secure with edible glue.

3. For the coat, roll out some Poppy MMP and cut out a rectangle measuring 9 x 3cm. Pleat the top end and wrap around the body with the join at the front.

4. Prepare the legs in the usual way. For the trouser legs, cut out two 5 x 4cm rectangles of Black SFP. Fold up the lower edge for the turn-up and wrap around the leg, trimming any excess paste from the back. Cut and neaten at the top of the leg, then glue to the body.

5. Cut a tiny strip of Black SFP for the purse strap and drape over his shoulder. Trim at the front and glue into place. Cut out a 1.5cm black square, fold in half and glue to the strap. Make two indents with a small CelStick.

6. Model the arms from cylinders of Poppy MMP. Hollow out one end with a bone tool and insert paws.

7. Attach a strip of Black SFP to the bear's head in front of one ear, under the chin and above the other ear.

8. Flatten a pea-sized piece of Poppy MMP for the hat and attach to the head.

9. Push the head into position, securing with edible glue.

10. Make three buttons using the button tool and secure in place.

Medium Bear

Make the second bear following the same method as for the large bear using 40g of mid brown MMP.

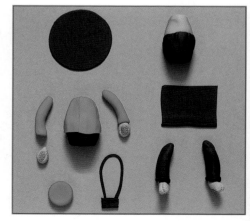

Babe in Arms

Materials

15 x 20cm/6 x 8" oval cake

910g/2lb white sugarpaste

SK Mexican Modelling Paste (MMP):

50g/1³/₄oz Rose

20g/³/₄oz Teddy Bear Brown

200g/7oz White

SK Paste Food Colours:
Cyclamen and Rose

SK Liquid Food Colour:
Blackberry

SK Metallic Lustre Dust Colour:
Snowflake

Royal icing

Equipment

23 x 28cm/9 x 11" oval cake
drum

Ceramic veining tool (HP)

Flower embossers: set 1 (HP)

Garrett frill cutter, centre
removed (OP)

Greaseproof paper

Piping bags

Piping nozzles:
nos. 1 and 43

Toy cutter set
(FMM)

Varipin (OP)

Method

1. Cover the board with white sugarpaste and texture with a
    varipin.

2. Cover the cake and place it on the board towards the
    back.

3. Wrap a strip of greaseproof paper around the cake and
    mark the circumference of the cake on the paper. Fold the
    strip into six equal sections. With the paper folded, cut a
    template for the scallops on the side of the cake.

4. Mix Rose and Cyclamen Paste Food Colours into some
    royal icing to achieve a dusky pink colour. Place a no. 1
    nozzle into a piping bag and fill with the pink royal icing.
    Pipe a dot and line design above the scallop template, then
    remove the template from the cake.

5. Blend 50g of Rose MMP with 50g of White MMP. Roll out

36

a small amount and cut out six rabbits. Dust with Snowflake Metallic Lustre Dust and paint the eyes and noses. Glue to the cake in the scallops.

6. Pipe a shell border around the cake.

7. Make the christening bears (see below) and position on the cake.

To Finish

1. Make a tiny toy bear using the stage

work as a guide. Paint the features with Blackberry Liquid Food Colour.

2. Make a blanket, bib and tiny slippers to lay on the board.

Christening Bears

Mix together 15g of Teddy Bear Brown MMP and 100g of White MMP to make a pale brown. Prepare a large and a small head.

Mummy Bear

1. Model the body and legs using mid brown MMP for the pads.

2. Cut out two Garrett frills from the pink MMP. Cover one with plastic film.

3. Frill one of the Garrett frills with a ceramic veiner and emboss the edge with a blossom tool. Cut a cross in the centre. Ease over the body and glue into place. Repeat the same method with the second layer.

4. Use pea-sized pieces of pink MMP for the puff sleeves. Roll into cones and hollow out the wide end with a bone tool. Mark

from the inside out with a blade tool.

5. Make the arms from the pale brown paste, attach to the sleeves and position on the body.

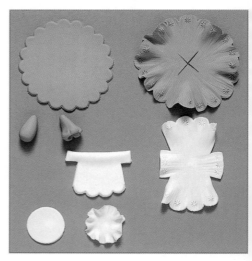

Baby Bear

1. Mould a long cone from 8g of the pale brown MMP. Glue the prepared head into the wide end.

2. Cut a rectangle of white paste measuring 14 x 7cm. Frill with a ceramic veining tool. Cut a strip for the trim 14cm x 1cm, frill and attach.

3. Pleat along the top edge, flatten with the large CelStick and re-trim. Wrap around the body with the join at the back.

4. Model two tiny arms.

5. Cut out four 3cm circles from White MMP. Frill one of the circles for the collar, fold in half and cut out the top with the end of a piping nozzle. Emboss with a blossom tool and attach to the dress.

6. Frill the other two circles for the bonnet and attach.

7. Make a bib from the remaining circle and secure in place.

6. Cut out a white Garrett frill, fold in half, then cut 1cm down and 1cm across to make a pinafore. Open out, frill and emboss with blossoms.

7. Frill a 3cm White MMP circle for the collar and secure in place. Reopen the top of the body with a CelStick.

8. For the hat, roll 10g of the pink MMP into a ball. Flatten the underneath, keeping the top rounded, then mark the edge with a blade tool.

9. Cut, frill and pleat a pink strip 18 x 2cm. Attach to the inside of the hat around the top. Repeat this method with a strip 10 x 2cm for the lower part of the hat. Mark stitching around the back of the hat.

10. Glue the hat to the head and twist the head into the body. Make and attach two pink ribbons.

11. Dust the dresses and bonnet with Snowflake Metallic Lustre Dust before the paste dries.

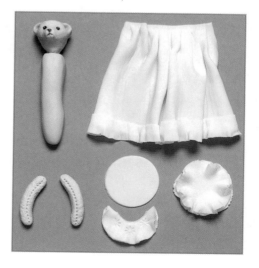

The Big Day

Materials

20 x 15cm/8 x 6" oval cake

910g/2lb white sugarpaste

SK Mexican Modelling Paste
(MMP):

15g/$\frac{1}{2}$oz Slate Grey

20g/$\frac{3}{4}$oz Teddy Bear Brown

150g/5oz White

SK Sugar Florist Paste (SFP):

10g/$\frac{1}{4}$oz Black

10g/$\frac{1}{4}$oz Holly/Ivy

10g/$\frac{1}{4}$oz White

SK Paste Food
Colours: Berberis
and Holly/Ivy

SK Metallic Lustre
Dust Colour:
Snowflake

Royal icing

Equipment

23 x 28cm/9 x 11" oval cake
drum

Bow cutter: small (JC)

Button tools (PME)

Ceramic veining tool (HP)

Flower embossers: set 1 (HP)

Garrett frill cutter, centre
removed (OP)

Piping bag

Piping nozzle: no. 43

Varipin (OP)

Method

1. Cover the board with white sugarpaste and texture with a varipin.

2. Cover the cake and position it centrally on the board.

3. Using white royal icing in a bag with a no. 43 nozzle, pipe a shell design around the bottom edge of the cake. Leave to firm.

4. Attach orange ribbon above the piping, securing at the back with a little royal icing.

Rose Buds and Leaves

1. Blend some Berberis Paste Food Colour into 10g of White SFP to create an orange colour. Make approximately 14 tiny rose buds using the same method as described in Ballet Dreams (see page 15).

2. Model approximately 16 tiny pointed leaves from Holly/Ivy SFP. Mark the veins with a Dresden tool.

To Finish

Make the wedding bears (see below) and place on top of the cake.

Wedding Bears

Blend 15g of Teddy Bear Brown MMP with 100g of White MMP to make a pale brown colour. Prepare two large heads.

Groom

1. Model a large body and legs using mid brown MMP for the pads.

2. Cut out a white collar using the template (page 48) and glue in position with the join at the front.

3. Roll out some Slate Grey MMP and cut out the waistcoat using the template (page 48). Run a stitching wheel around the edge. Wrap around the bear, overlapping the paste at the front.

4. Make the arms in the usual way and glue in place.

5. Make two buttons using the button tool and secure to the waistcoat.

6. Cut out a bow tie from Black SFP and glue into place.

7. Cut one ear off the bear's head. For his hat, roll a pea-sized piece of Slate Grey MMP into a ball. Flatten out with your thumb, leaving a ridge on the outside edge. Attach a slightly flattened ball to the centre and mark a small ridge with your finger.

8. Attach a thin strip of black to the hat. Glue the hat to the head before twisting the finished head into the body.

9. Blend some Holy/Ivy Paste Food Colour into royal icing. Snip a small hole in the tip of a piping bag and pipe two tiny leaves for the button hole. Attach a tiny rose bud (see above) while the icing is wet.

Bride

1. Make the bride's body and legs in the same way as for the groom.

2. Cut out a Garrett frill from White MMP. Frill and emboss around the edge with

7. Cut out a veil from White MMP using the template (page 48). Texture with a veiner and emboss the bottom edge. Pleat along the top edge, flatten with a CelStick and re-cut. Glue into position, folding under the bottom edge and draping the paste to give movement. Dust the veil with Snowflake.

8. Take a pea-sized piece of Holly/Ivy SFP and mould a flattened cone shape. Drape over her paws.

blossoms. Cut a cross in the centre and ease over the body.

3. Mould cones of White MMP, indent the wide ends and mark with a blade tool to create frilly sleeves.

4. Make the arms from pale brown MMP. Glue to the sleeves and attach to the body. Glue the paws together in front of the bear. This will help to hold the flower spray in place.

5. Cut out a 5cm circle from White MMP for the collar, frill and emboss with blossoms. Attach to the body and reopen the top with a CelStick. Dust the dress with Snowflake Metallic Lustre Dust.

6. Glue the head into position and leave to firm.

9. Pipe an arrangement of tiny leaves for the headdress and position six buds and leaves. Pipe and arrange remaining buds and leaves for her flower bouquet. Dust the flowers with Snowflake.

White Christmas

Materials

20cm/8" round cake

910g/2lb white sugarpaste

SK Mexican Modelling Paste (MMP)

20g/³/₄oz Pale Mint

50g/1³/₄oz Poppy

200g/7oz White

50g/1³/₄oz Wisteria

SK Metallic Lustre Dust Colour: Snowflake

Royal icing

Caster sugar

Equipment

28cm/11" round cake drum

Bow cutter: small (JC)

Button tool (HP)

Method

1. Cover the board with white sugarpaste and emboss with texture mats.

2. Cover the cake and texture the top and sides in the same way.

3. Stipple white royal icing with a brush and firm sponge around the bottom edge of the cake and the edge of the top surface.

4. Whilst the royal icing is still soft, sprinkle with caster sugar. Shake off the excess then leave to dry.

5. Brush the cake and board with Snowflake Metallic Lustre Dust.

6. Make the Christmas bears (see page 46) and place on top of the cake.

To Finish

Make snowballs from White MMP, brush with edible glue and dip in caster sugar. Lay around the board and cake.

44

Christmas Bears

Prepare two large, one medium and one small head from White MMP.

Mummy Christmas

1. Model the body from 25g of White MMP.

2. Make the legs from 10g of White MMP.

3. Roll two pea-sized pieces of Poppy MMP into sausage shapes for the boots. Hollow out one end with a bone tool and glue to each leg. Bend up the foot and mark the heel with a blade tool.

4. Roll out some Poppy MMP and cut out the skirt using the template (page 48). Pleat along the top edge and attach to the body with the join at the back.

5. Cut out the coat template (page 48) from Poppy MMP. Pleat along the top edge, flatten with a CelStick and re-cut. Fold in the sides and bottom edge. Wrap around the body giving the paste movement as you do so and joining at the front.

6. Roll a sausage of paste to fit inside the arm template (page 48). Bend up and mark creases in the arms.

7. Flatten a tiny sausage of White MMP between two texture mats for the muff. Glue at the back, cutting off any excess paste. Secure the arms firmly to the body.

8. Roll out a 5cm circle for the collar and cut a 2cm circle from the centre. Cut and round off the front. Make three pleats and attach in place.

9. For the hat, mould a large pea-sized ball of paste into an oval. Flatten slightly and make a ridge around the edge with your thumb. Flatten an oval for the centre. Cut one ear off the bear's head and glue the hat to the head before attaching the finished head to the body.

10. Cut a strip of Wisteria MMP for the trim and make three tiny rose buds (see Ballet Dreams, page 15). Make some tiny leaves from Pale Mint MMP. Attach the buds and leaves to the hat. Finish off the muff with leaves and berries.

11. Cut out a bow from Wisteria MMP and attach to the front of the coat.

12. Make the trim for the collar and coat by

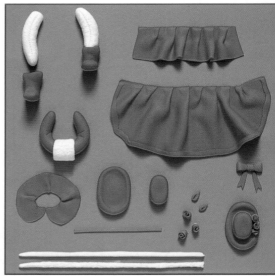

rolling cylinders of White MMP between the texture mats. Secure in place with edible glue.

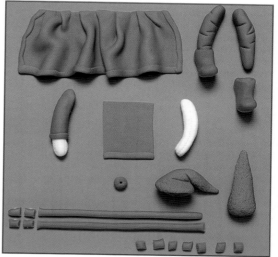

Daddy Christmas

1. Model the body from 25g of White MMP.

2. For the trouser legs, mould two cylinders from 10g of Wisteria MMP and mark creases with a blade tool.

3. Make boots as before and glue to the legs.

4. Make a coat from Wisteria MMP using the template (page 48). Pleat the top edge, flatten and re-cut. Fold in the sides and bottom edge. Wrap around the bear with the join left over right at the front.

5. Model the arms from White MMP. Cut out coat sleeves using the template (page 48). Fold over the bottom edge for the cuff. Attach to the arm with the join at the side. Trim any excess paste from the top and fold inwards. Mark a bend in the arms and attach to the body.

6. To make the hat, roll 10g of Wisteria MMP into a cone between the texture mats. Ball out the wide end, bend the top down and mark creases. Cut one ear off the bear and glue the hat on the head. Twist the head into place, then attach a bobble on the hat.

7. To make a scarf, roll two long cylinders of Poppy and Pale Mint MMP, cut into tiny pieces and stick together with cooled, boiled water, alternating the colours (edible glue is too tacky for this purpose). Roll this between the texture mats, cut to the required length and cut tassels on the ends. Wrap around the bear, draping it over his shoulder.

8. Cut out two tiny pockets from Pale Mint MMP, attach one to his arm, bending down the edge, and one on the coat. Mark stitching with a small CelStick.

Little Christmas Bears

Using the sizing guides (inside front cover), make a medium and a small bear from White MMP. Using the same method as for the other Christmas bears, give them hats and scarves in Wisteria, Pale Mint and Poppy MMP.

47

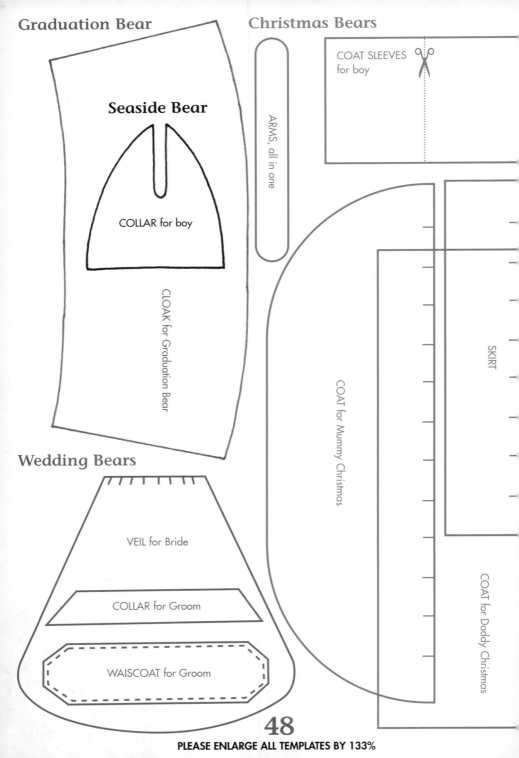

Graduation Bear

Seaside Bear

Christmas Bears

COLLAR for boy

COAT SLEEVES for boy

ARMS, all in one

CLOAK for Graduation Bear

COAT for Mummy Christmas

SKIRT

COAT for Daddy Christmas

Wedding Bears

VEIL for Bride

COLLAR for Groom

WAISCOAT for Groom

48

PLEASE ENLARGE ALL TEMPLATES BY 133%